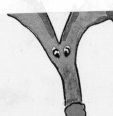

This book has
been donated

WELCOME
BACK TO
SCHOOL!

The BIGGEST and BRIGHTEST LIGHT

A True Story of the Heart

by Marilyn Perlyn · illustrated by Amanda Perlyn
foreword by Muhammad Ali

Robert D. Reed Publishers

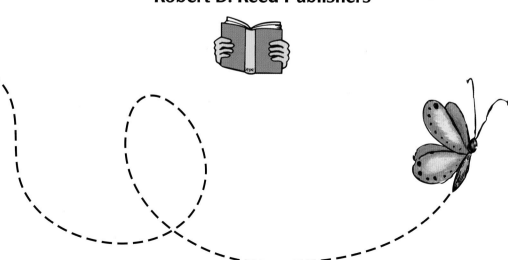

Text copyright © 2004 by Marilyn Perlyn
Illustrations copyright © 2004 by Amanda Perlyn
Foreword copyright © 2004 by Muhammad Ali

Published by **Robert D. Reed Publishers**

1380 Face Rock Drive,
Bandon, Oregon 97411
Phono (541) 347-9882
Fax (541) 347-9883
E-mail 4bobreed@msn.com
www.rdrpublishers.com

Printed in China

10 9 8 7 6 5 4 3

Library of Congress Cataloging-in-Publication Data
Perlyn, Marilyn.
   The biggest and brightest light : a true story of the
heart / by Marilyn Perlyn ; illustrated by Amanda
Perlyn : foreword by Muhammad Ali
   p. cm.
   SUMMARY: When six-year-old Amanda wanted to help her
teacher who had a problem, she wondered what she could
do. She thought of making holiday decorations, baking
cookies, or entering a contest. Through her efforts to
help her teacher, Amanda discovered that helping others
gave her the best feeling she ever had.
   Audience: Ages 4-8.
   ISBN 1-931741-30-1

   1. Helping behavior in children--Juvenile literature.
2. Thoughtfulness--Juvenile literature. [1. Helpfulness.
2. Thoughtfulness. 3. Conduct of life.]   I. Perlyn,
Amanda. II. Title.

BF637.H4.P47 2004   177'.7
                   QB103-700390

**To Elena,
for
whom the flowers
shall always
bloom.**

To Dr. Marguerite Malko,
Amanda's first grade teacher,
who shared her knowledge
and her heart with
her students.

To Rose Nash,
whose inspiration and guidance
helped Amanda create the
splendid artwork
in this book.

Foreword

In 1996 I had the honor of lighting the Centennial Olympic Flame in Atlanta, Georgia. This is a light that is celebrated throughout the world. Just as the Olympic torch passes from person to person, over mountains and seas, may each of your acts of caring kindle a light in another to reach out and make a difference in someone's life. It is my hope that this story, *The Biggest and Brightest Light*, will be the spirit that sparks that desire.

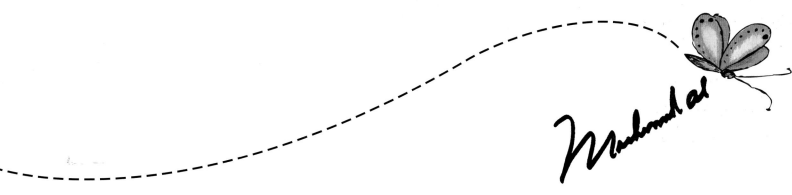

Muhammad Ali

Amanda felt the warm, soothing heat of the sun on her worried face. It was the last day of summer. The mailman had delivered a letter that said Amanda's teacher for the new school year was Dr. Malko. She wondered if her teacher was a doctor, did that mean that she was going to get a shot tomorrow?

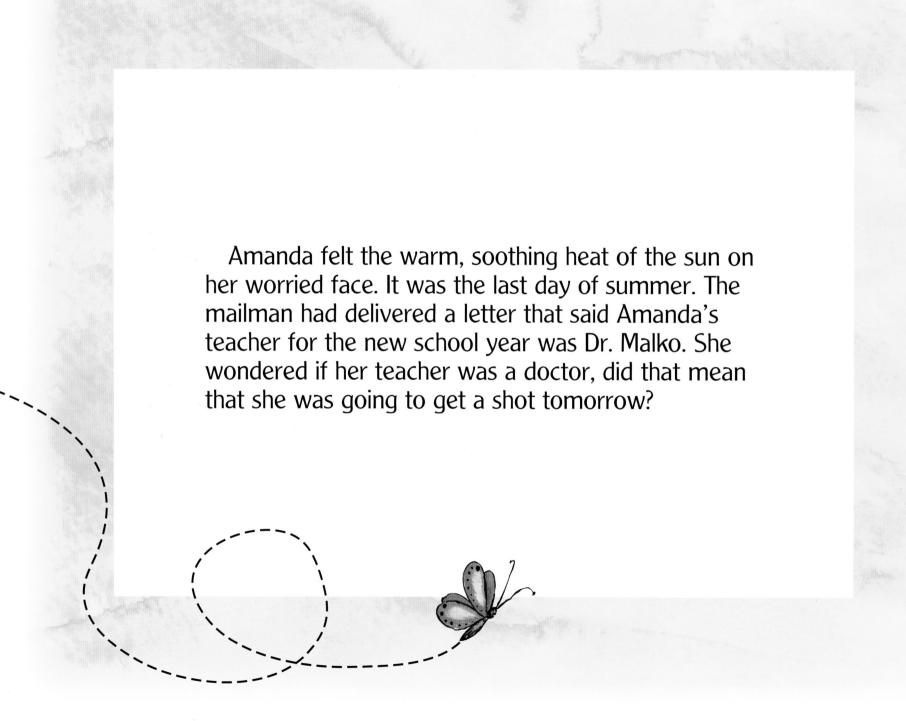

"Hi, I'm Dr. Malko," said Amanda's teacher as the children entered the classroom. Dr. Malko was a tall lady with a cheerful smile.

"Boys and girls," said Dr. Malko, "today we are going to get to know one another. My name is on the blackboard. I want to explain to you that I am not a doctor of medicine. I am a doctor of education. That means I received extra training as a teacher. Don't worry, I won't ask you to stick out your tongues and say, 'AHHHH!'" All the students laughed.

"I have two grown-up children," said Dr. Malko. "My daughter, Elena, lives nearby and my son, Michael, lives far away. Now I would like each of you to tell us about yourself."

Amanda giggled as she said, "I have two brothers and two pets. My new puppy is very playful but my brothers are scared to play with Baby Monster, my pet iguana. He's really big with horns on his nose and spikes on his back."

Everyone wanted to hear more about Amanda's iguana but it was time for Dr. Malko to hand out the schoolbooks.

Of all the things she loved at school, Amanda liked story time the best. Each day the children gathered in a circle to listen as Dr. Malko read from their favorite books. *Guess My Hat* was the book Amanda enjoyed the most.

"My job is helping people. I ride on a fast truck that has ladders and hoses. Can you guess my hat?" asked Dr. Malko as she read to the children.

Before anyone could speak, Amanda shouted, "It's a firefighter's hat!"

At the end of the story, the boys and girls each chose a hat to wear from the hat box. Suddenly, one classmate became a baker, one a nurse, one a painter, until the hat box was completely empty.

After story time, Amanda's second favorite activity was art. In October, instead of the usual craft project, Dr. Malko helped the children make pumpkin cookies. Amanda decorated her cookie with orange icing and black sprinkles. She licked the icing and grinned as she thought about her Halloween costume. She was going to dress up as a wicked witch with ugly, rotten teeth and a giant wart on her nose.

The day after Halloween, the jack-o-lantern was erased from the blackboard and a big, fat turkey took its place.

"Today we are going to begin practicing for the Thanksgiving play. We will start by learning an old rhyme that goes like this," said Dr. Malko.

A turkey is a funny bird.
His head goes wobble, wobble.
But all he says is just one word,
"Gobble, gobble, gobble."

The children loved the rhyme so much that they repeated it over and over, until they learned it in no time at all.

After lunch, Amanda noticed that Dr. Malko looked like she didn't feel well. Her face was sad and her lips were pale.

"My daughter, Elena, is very sick," Dr. Malko finally told the children. She tried very hard to put on a smile, but they all knew that she was worried.

The next day Amanda heard the other teachers saying that Dr. Malko needed extra money for Elena's doctor's bills. Amanda knew that she could not make Elena well but maybe she could find a way to help Dr. Malko.

She wondered what she could do. Maybe she could have a bake sale or a lemonade stand. She thought and she thought . . . then she thought some more . . . until a great idea came to her.

"I could make Christmas decorations, sell them, and give the money to Dr. Malko," she said to herself. After a few days of hard work, with the help of her mother, the holiday decorations were ready.

"Red-nosed reindeer . . . only ten dollars!" Amanda shouted as people lined up to buy them.

One hundred reindeer were sold and Amanda collected one thousand dollars!

Amanda's mom brought the money to school the following day so Amanda could give it to Dr. Malko. Dr. Malko could not believe her eyes when Amanda handed her all of that money!

"This money is going to help me so much. You know, Amanda, when children do such special deeds, they are like angels with invisible halos on their heads. Thank you, my little angel," said Dr. Malko.

It was the proudest moment of Amanda's life! Helping someone else gave her the best feeling that she had ever, *ever* had. It was better than eating a big chocolate sundae, better than opening up all the presents at her birthday party, and it was even better than the day she got her new wet-nosed puppy!

Christmas was coming soon. The children made popcorn garlands for the Christmas tree and hung them, along with strands of twinkling, colored lights that decorated the room. The Hannukah menorah and Kwanzaa candles were set up and each day another light was lit.

The holiday lights were magical. Their bright twinkle gave Amanda a warm and special feeling inside. She knew her house would soon be filled with the delicious smells of Mama's cooking. The table would be set with the prettiest dishes. Family and friends would gather to be together and, of course, there would be all those wonderful presents to open!

One of the best presents that Amanda received came from Dr. Malko and Elena when they visited her during the Christmas vacation. Amanda was so happy to meet Elena.

"We brought you a special gift to show our appreciation for your kindness," said Dr. Malko. She handed Amanda a big box, wrapped in shiny red paper with a bright gold ribbon on it.

Amanda opened the box, peeked inside, and quickly pulled out two of the most adorable teddy bears. They felt as soft as the fur on a bunny rabbit.

"They're so cute," screamed Amanda, as she leaned over to hug Dr. Malko and Elena.

The children returned to school after the holiday vacation. Amanda wasn't very patient as she listened to her friends talk about their new toys.

"I got a new doll and two teddy bears," Amanda blurted out with a big smile.

The morning bell rang and it was time to begin the day.

Amanda came home from school that day feeling very blue. While her mother was making dinner, she and Amanda talked.

"Mommy," said Amanda, "Dr. Malko told us that Elena had to go to the hospital because she is even sicker than she was before. I'm sad that Dr. Malko can't spend very much time with Elena."

Amanda was only six years old, but she knew how much all kids need their mom or dad when they are sick.

Amanda really wanted to bake cookies for Elena, but Dr. Malko told her that Elena was on a special diet and couldn't eat them. What could she do? She thought and she thought . . . and she thought some more . . . until another great idea came to her.

"My mommy and I made these cookies for you to bring to the hospital," said Amanda, as she handed Dr. Malko a big basket of the most delicious smelling double chocolate chip cookies.

Attached to the basket was a note that read:

> Dear Nurses,
>   Elena's mom can't be with her because she is at school teaching my class. Please enjoy some cookies and be a mom to Elena until Dr. Malko returns.
>   Amanda

Amanda felt so good to know that even something as simple as cookies would help to put smiles on the faces of Elena and her mom. The next day Amanda received a very special note from Dr. Malko.

The saddest day of all came when Dr. Malko was called to the hospital. The doctor said that Elena really needed her.

When she got there, Dr. Malko told Elena how very much she loved her. She sat and prayed, holding her daughter's hand. She stayed by her side until she died.

Although there was nothing more she could do for Elena, Dr. Malko sat quietly for a while before leaving the hospital.

Even though it was hard, Dr. Malko returned to school the next day.

"Children," sighed Dr. Malko, "I have something very, very sad to tell you."

The children's eyes quickly filled with tears. Amanda reached for a tissue as a tear rolled down her cheek.

The boys and girls decided to plant a beautiful tree with bright yellow flowers in the garden outside of their classroom. Amanda and her classmates helped to dig the hole and shovel the dirt around the tree.

Each child said something special that warmed Dr. Malko's heart.

"I hope that this tree will grow tall and strong," said Amanda, "and that its beautiful yellow blooms will always remind us of Elena."

The months passed quickly as the rainy days of April turned into the sunny days of May. The warmer days meant school was almost over.

As a special treat, Dr. Malko allowed the boys and girls to bring their pets to school on the last day of class. Ink, the Dalmatian puppy, was the cutest pet with a big black spot over one eye. Hilda and Matilda, the twin goldfish, were the smallest pets. But the most unusual pet was Amanda's iguana. While the children ate their pizza, Baby Monster munched on his lunch of a hibiscus flower.

When it was time to say goodbye, the children and Dr. Malko talked about how much they would miss each other.

"Dr. Malko, you're the very best teacher! I will never forget you," said Amanda.

Amanda was excited that summer was finally here. She was getting ready to go away for a vacation with her family. She was packing the two small teddy bears that Dr. Malko and Elena had given her. As she picked them up, she thought she heard the bears' small voices whisper to her,

"Happy, happy is the day
when you help someone
in a special way."

Amanda listened closely and nodded her head. Then she carefully put the bears in her suitcase and left for her trip.

After a great summer visiting her cousins, Amanda was ready to get back to school. She stopped by Dr. Malko's classroom to give her a hug and ask her how her summer had been.

"I brought you a present, Dr. Malko," said Amanda, as she handed her a big red ceramic apple with a plant in it.

"Thank you, Amanda. This is very special to me," said Dr. Malko as she put the plant on her desk.

Amanda's mommy picked her up from school. They went shopping for school supplies and new shoes. At the store they saw a sign for a special holiday contest. The contest rules read, "Describe in 100 words or less why you wish someone could be with you for the holidays . . . and your wish may come true!" Even though it was a long time away, the winning prize was a free airplane ticket to be used at Christmas time.

"Why don't you enter the contest?" asked Amanda's mom. "It would be great if you could win the airplane ticket for Dr. Malko. Then she could be with her son, Michael, for the holidays. Otherwise, it will be lonely for her without Elena."

"I'm too little to win," answered Amanda.

"Oh, go ahead. You'll never know unless you try," replied her mother.

"What would I write about?" asked Amanda.

She thought and she thought . . . and she thought some more . . . until still another great idea came to her. She picked up a contest application and wrote about her special wish.

Wish You WERE HERE!

OFFICIAL ENTRY FORM

Describe why you wish someone could be here for the holidays and... Your wish may just come true!

I am writing in this contest because I think the world would be a better place if people showed each other how much they care. I want to show my 1st grade teacher, Dr. Malko, how much I love and care about her. Her daughter died this year. All she has left is her son, Michael, who lives in Idaho. For all her hard work teaching kids her whole life, I think she deserves to have Christmas with her only family. I think if you believe a wish will come true it might really happen. I got a fortune cookie that said, "An emptiness will soon be filled." Now I want to give my fortune to Dr. Malko!

Just before Christmas, Amanda received a very special phone call. She listened with excitement as she heard the lady on the phone say, "Amanda, your wish has come true! You won the contest for your teacher! Dr. Malko will now be able to spend the holiday with her son. We are all very proud of you!"

It was too good to be true! Could a child win something so special for her teacher? The answer was yes! No matter how old you are, you are old enough to make a difference in someone's life.

The day arrived when Dr. Malko was leaving to visit Michael. Amanda and her mommy went to the airport. As the wheels of the plane left the ground, Amanda waved goodbye to her teacher.

"Mommy, look at the tiny blue lights on the runway," said Amanda, as she pressed her nose against the airport window. She watched as the big jet soared towards the stars. The stars seemed to shimmer in the nighttime sky. They reminded her of the magical lights of the Christmas season that she loved so much.

Amanda glowed with pride. She closed her eyes for a moment and pictured the thousands of twinkling lights. However, she knew . . .

The day arrived when Dr. Malko was leaving to visit Michael. Amanda and her mommy went to the airport. As the wheels of the plane left the ground, Amanda waved goodbye to her teacher.

"Mommy, look at the tiny blue lights on the runway," said Amanda, as she pressed her nose against the airport window. She watched as the big jet soared towards the stars. The stars seemed to shimmer in the nighttime sky. They reminded her of the magical lights of the Christmas season that she loved so much.

Amanda glowed with pride. She closed her eyes for a moment and pictured the thousands of twinkling lights. However, she knew . . .

. . . that as long as she remembered the teddy bears' message, *the biggest and brightest light* would always be in her heart.

Amanda Perlyn and Dr. Marguerite Malko

A portion of the proceeds from this book will be donated to
The Heart of America Foundation to honor and recognize
kids under twelve who have made a difference in the lives of others
through their acts of caring. If you have a story of the heart
that you would like to share, please write or email:
The Heart of America Foundation
Gee Whiz Kids
401 F Street, NW, Suite 325
Washington, DC 20001
Email: heartofam@aol.com